Adventure Book

THIRD EDITION

KENDALL/HUNT PUBLISHING COMPANY
4050 Westmark Drive Dubuque, Iowa 52002

A TIMS® Curriculum
University of Illinois at Chicago

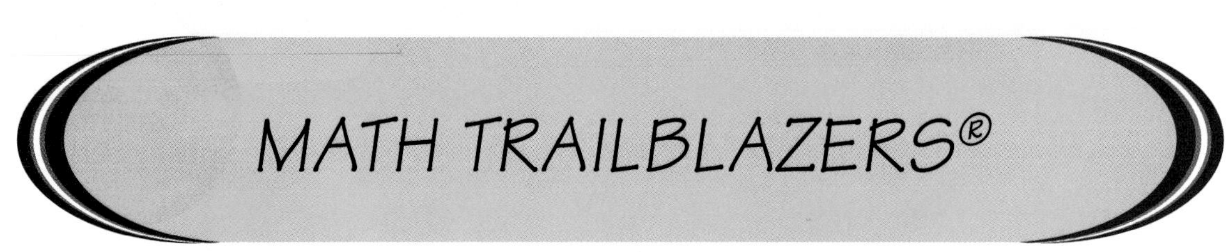

Dedication

This book is dedicated to
the children and teachers who
let us see the magic in their classrooms
and to our families who wholeheartedly
supported us while we searched for
ways to make it happen.

The TIMS Project

UIC The University of Illinois at Chicago

The original edition was based on work supported by the National Science Foundation under grant No. MDR 9050226 and the University of Illinois at Chicago. Any opinions, findings, and conclusions or recommendations expressed in this publication are those of the authors and do not necessarily reflect the views of the granting agencies.

ISBN 978-0-7575-3493-5

Printed in the United States of America

1 2 3 4 5 6 7 8 9 10 11 10 09 08 07

Table of Contents

The Four Servants

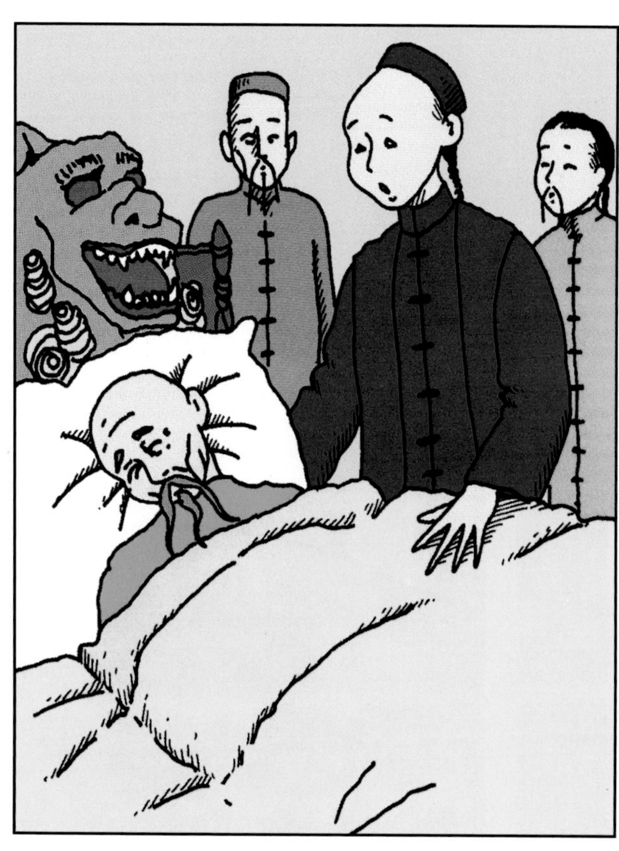

Once there was a king who was very sick, so sick he was about to die. All the wise men and women of the kingdom agreed that only the golden bird's singing could save him. But no one knew where to find the golden bird.

Now the king had a son who loved his father dearly. "I will find the golden bird," said the prince.

So the young prince set out to find the golden bird and save his father's life.

Before long the prince came upon a girl with a pencil in her hand. The girl was surrounded by papers filled with beautiful drawings.

"What are you doing?" asked the prince.

"I am drawing pictures," answered the girl. "I can draw anything so that it looks as real as life. Do you think I could be of use to you as a servant?"

"What a wonderful skill!" said the prince. "Come along and follow me. Who knows if drawing pictures may not be useful?"

And so Artist followed the prince as his servant.

Before long they came upon a fellow who was also surrounded by papers. These papers were filled with tables of data.

"What are you doing, sir?" asked the prince.

"Why, I am taking data and organizing it into tables," replied the fellow. "Give me any amount of information and I will sort it out and organize it in a data table. Could you use a fellow like me?"

"Come along," said the prince. "Who knows if table-making may not be useful?"

And so Table-Maker followed the prince too.

A little farther along they came upon yet another fellow surrounded by papers. But these papers were filled with numbers, lines, and points.

"Who are you and what are you doing?" asked the prince.

"I am making graphs," replied this fellow. "Give me any data and I will graph it so that anyone can understand it. Do you think you could use a fellow like me as a servant?"

"Why not?" replied the prince. "Who knows but that graphing might not be useful?"

And so Grapher joined the others following the prince.

Yet a little farther along the prince saw a girl lying on the grass looking up into the sky.

"What are you doing?" asked the prince.

"What an easy question!" answered the girl. "I was just thinking about some hard questions. How many clouds are in the sky? I love to answer hard questions. Could you use someone like me for a servant?"

"Why not?" said the prince. "Who knows when we might need to have a hard question answered? In truth, I have a hard question right now. Where can I find the golden bird?"

"I don't know where the golden bird is," said Answerer, "but we could ask Mother Hollah for help. I have heard that she is the wisest woman in the land."

So the prince set off to see Mother Hollah. Artist, Table-Maker, Grapher, and Answerer followed. When they arrived at Mother Hollah's hut, the old woman was waiting for them.

"So, you are looking for the golden bird," said Mother Hollah. "If you can solve my puzzle, then I will tell you where to find the golden bird. My puzzle is, 'How tall is the giant who made this handprint?'"

And Mother Hollah showed the prince and his servants a huge handprint.

"What a monster that giant must be!" exclaimed the prince. "How are we ever to find how tall such a creature is?"

But Artist was already at work.

"Look here," she said. "I have drawn the giant, whose height we don't know, and the handprint, which is here in front of us. We want to know the height, *H*. We can measure the length of the hand print, *L*."

"That's true," said the prince. "We have to find the giant's height. We can measure the length of the handprint, but will that help us find the height?"

Table-Maker had an idea. "Let's gather some data. We will measure the length of our hands and our height. We'll organize our data in a table. Maybe that will tell us something, but even if it doesn't, we'll have fun!"

"Good idea, Table-Maker," said the prince.

So the prince and his four servants began to make measurements. To find their heights, they worked in pairs. One in each pair stood against a wall, and the other used a meterstick to measure the height.

To measure the length of their handprints, first they traced their hands on paper. Then, they measured the lengths from the wrists to the middle fingertip.

So the prince and his four servants measured their heights and the lengths of their handprints.

"We should try to measure very big and very small people, too," said Table-Maker. "That will make any patterns in the data show up more clearly."

So the prince and his servants measured people on the road and in the village. They measured carefully because they knew the king's life depended on them.

Person	*L* Hand Length (cm)	*H* Height (cm)
Newborn	5	46
Baby Carrie	8	74
Toddler	10	92
Answerer	14	129
Prince	15	135
Shepherd Girl	16	148
Artist	16	150
Table-Maker	18	170
Grapher	20	183
Peddler Woman	21	191
Tall Man	25	223
Giant	50	

Finally, they measured the length of the giant's handprint. Table-Maker organized all the data in a table.

"That was fun," said the prince. "And this data table seems to be helping. But the pattern is not clear to me. I still don't know the giant's height."

"I can help," said Grapher. "I'll plot the data. Then maybe we'll understand better."

In a moment, Grapher had made a clear graph. He saw that the data points were close to a straight line, so he drew a straight line that fit the pattern of the points.

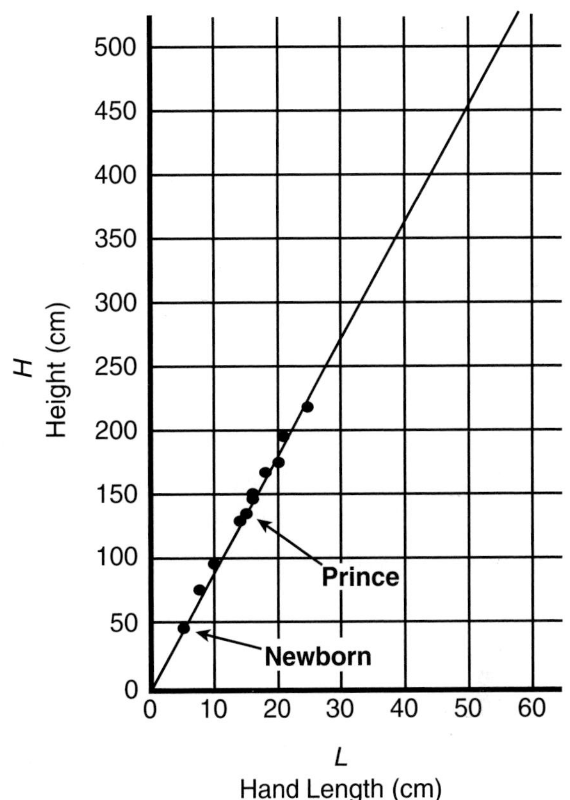

"I think this graph will help us answer Mother Hollah's riddle," said Answerer.

"Well, maybe," said the prince. "But I don't understand it. Can someone explain it to me?"

"The points on this graph stand for the people we measured," said Grapher. "See, this point is for you; your hand length is 15 cm and your height is 135 cm. This point here is for the newborn: hand length 5 cm and height 46 cm. Every point is for a person we measured."

"All right," said the prince, "but why did you draw a line?"

"The line shows where points for people we didn't measure would probably be," said Grapher.

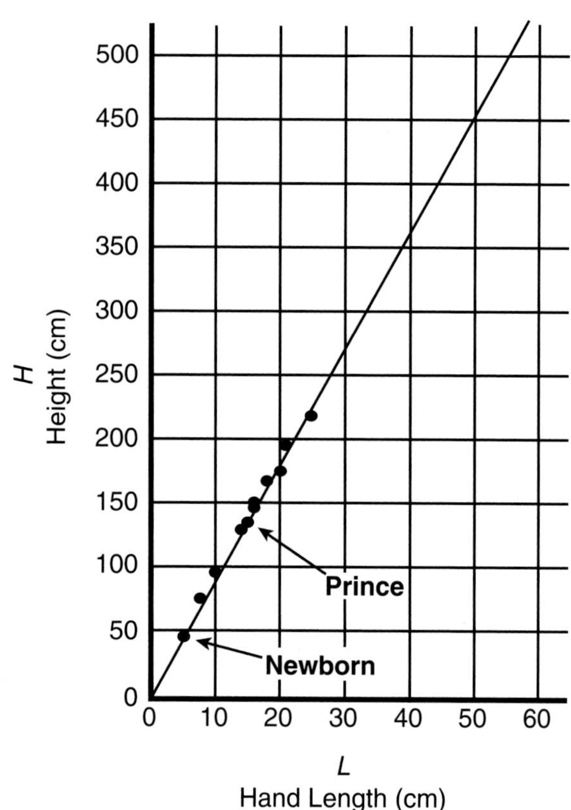

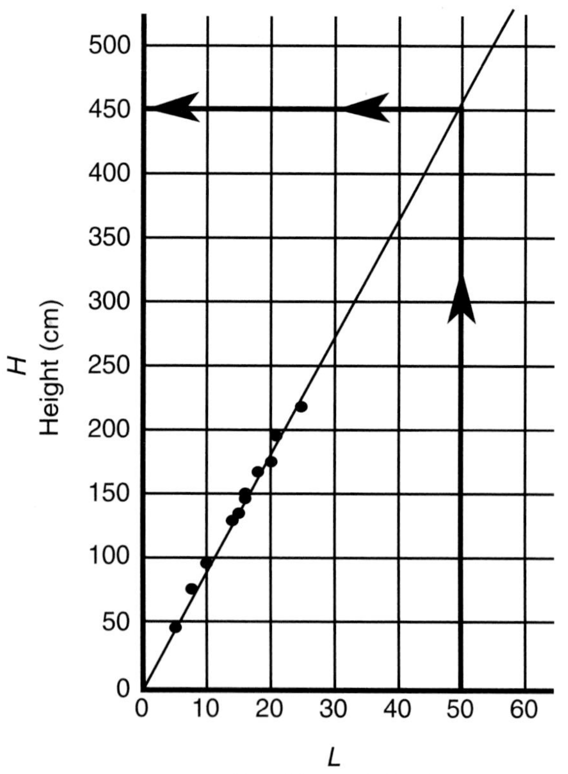

"I can see now that it's a very fine graph," said the prince, "but I still don't understand how it helps us find the giant's height."

"Look again," said Answerer. "Since all our points fall close to a line, the giant's point will be close to the line too. Since we know that the length of the giant's hand is 50 cm, we will use that to predict the height. Find L = 50 cm on the horizontal axis, go up to the best-fit line, and go over to the vertical axis. This shows us that the giant's height is probably about 450 cm."

"That's four and a half meters. That makes sense as a giant's height," said the prince, "but I would feel better if we could solve the problem in another way too."

"Good idea," said Answerer. "It's always better to solve an important problem another way. Tell me, Prince, do you see any patterns in our data table?"

"Well," said the prince, "it seems that when hand length gets bigger, so does height."

Person	*L* Hand Length (cm)	*H* Height (cm)
Newborn	5	46
Baby Carrie	8	74
Toddler	10	92
Answerer	14	129
Prince	15	135
Shepherd Girl	16	148
Artist	16	150
Table-Maker	18	170
Grapher	20	183
Peddler Woman	21	191
Tall Man	25	223
Giant	50	

"Very good," said Answerer, "but there's more of a pattern than just that. Look at the data in the hand length column for the newborn and for the toddler. What do you notice?"

"The toddler's hand is twice as long as the newborn's," answered the prince.

"Right," said Answerer. "Now, what about the height for the newborn and the toddler?"

"It looks as though the height about doubles, too," said the prince.

Answerer helped the prince find many patterns in the data table. The prince saw that when the length doubled or tripled, then the height usually did about the same.

"But how do all these data table patterns help us find the giant's height?" asked the prince.

"Look at the hand length for the Tall Man and the hand length for the giant. What do you notice about them?" asked Answerer.

Person	*L* Hand Length	*H* Height (cm)
Newborn	5	45
Baby Conic	8	74
Toddler	10	92
Answerer	14	120
Prince	15	135
Shepherd Girl	16	149
Artist	16	[illegible]
Table - Maker	18	[illegible]
Grapher	20	[illegible]
Peddler Woman	[illegible]	[illegible]
Tall Man	[illegible]	223
Giant	50	

"The hand length doubles," answered the prince. "So that means the height must double, too. That would make the giant about 446 cm tall. That's just about what we found from the graph."

"Yes," said Answerer. "But we can also estimate the giant's height by using other people we measured."

The prince and Answerer studied Table-Maker's table for a long time. All their estimates for the giant's height were close.

"Now I'm sure we're right," said the prince. "Let's tell Mother Hollah."

Mother Hollah smiled when the prince gave her the giant's height. "You have used your tools well to make a good prediction. Here is the giant. If you will measure her height, you will find that she is 448 cm tall."

"The golden bird is on top of the golden mountain," said Mother Hollah. "The way is far, but the giant will carry you."

The giant carried the prince to the golden mountain. There the prince found a golden cage and in it the golden bird. The prince took the bird and cage and returned to his father's kingdom. His four faithful servants went with him.

As soon as the bird came into the palace, it began to sing the most beautiful songs. Right away the king began to feel better. Before long he was stronger and healthier than ever.

Now the four servants were not idle either. They carried out many experiments and discovered many interesting and useful things. They helped to make the kingdom a rich and happy place.

After many years, the old king died and the prince became king. And if he hasn't died yet, why he's still king today!

Two Heads Are Better Than One

Ready, Domingo?
OK, Sharon.

That was 44 cm.

We dropped the ball from 40 cm and 80 cm.
Right. Now we have to drop it from 120 cm.

This time I'll drop and you watch.
It should go near 60 cm.

Tennis Ball

D Drop Height (in cm)	*B* Bounce Height (in cm)			
	Trial 1	Trial 2	Trial 3	Average
40	20	22	21	21
80	47	44	44	44
120	66	65	69	66

Now we have to graph the data and answer the questions.

We are supposed to predict the bounce height when the drop height is 60 cm. I get 33 cm.
I get 35 cm. Let's try it out.

OK. Ready.
It went to 34 cm. Good. We're both close.

Now we have to predict how high the ball will bounce if we drop it from 160 cm. We'll have to make the line longer.
That's extrapolation.

I extended the line,
and I got a bounce height of 88 cm.
Uh, oh. I get 75 cm.

13 cm is a big difference!
What's wrong?
Let's ask Mrs. Graham.

No. Let's work on it some more. We both have the same data, so we should get answers that are close.
Maybe it's the way we drew the line.

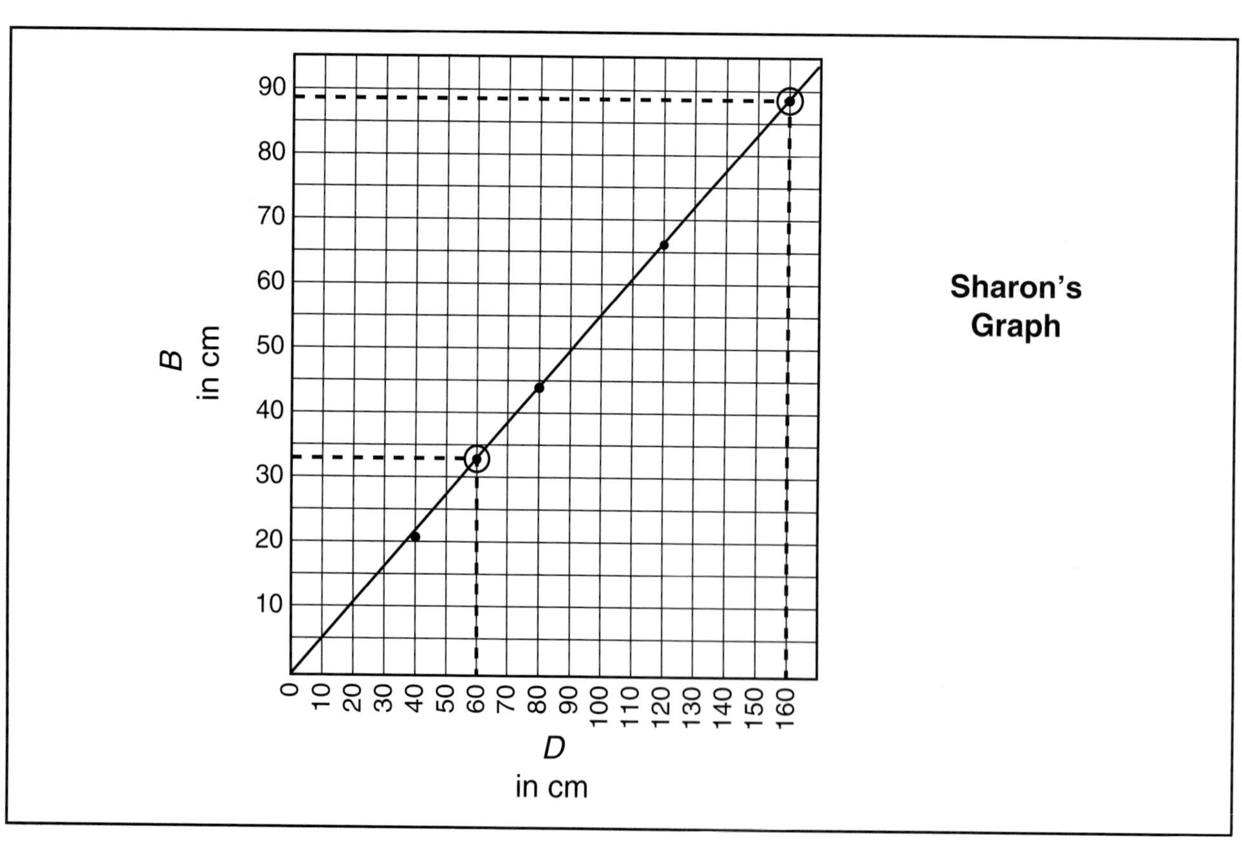
Sharon's Graph
B in cm
D in cm
90
80
70
60
50
40
30
20
10
0
10
20
30
40
50
60
70
80
90
100
110
120
130
140
150
160

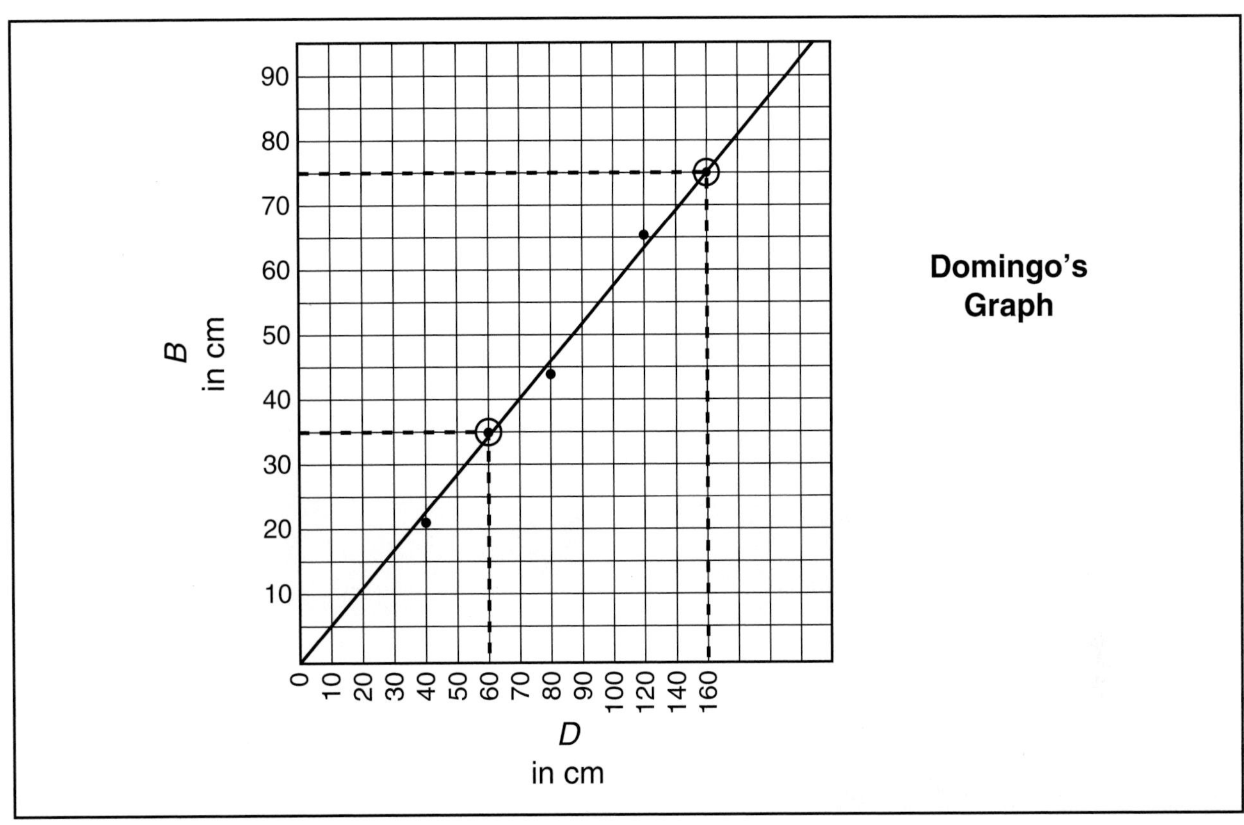
Domingo's Graph
B in cm
D in cm
10
20
30
40
50
60
70
80
90
0
10
20
30
40
50
60
70
80
90
100
120
140
160

Our lines fit our points OK. But my data is closer to the line than yours.
That's just the way I drew my line. It's different from yours.

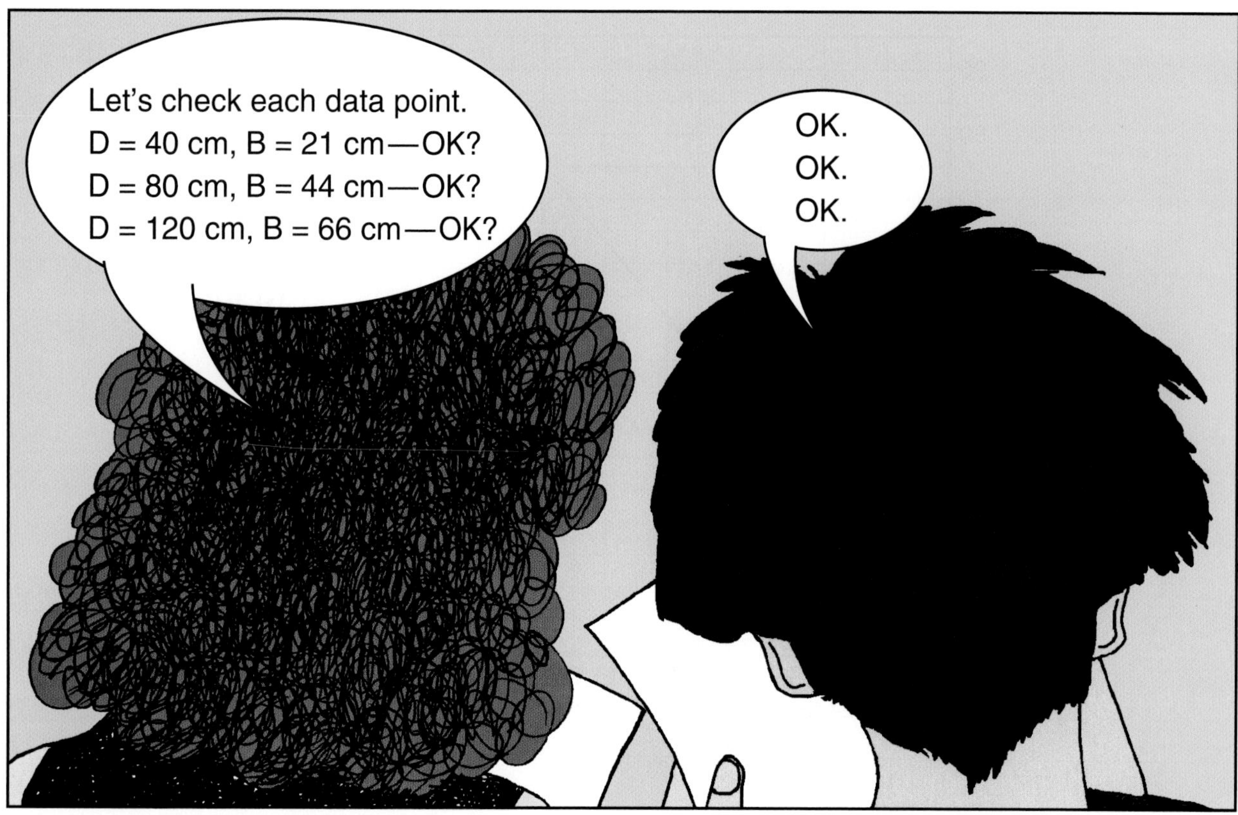
Let's check each data point.
D = 40 cm, B = 21 cm—OK?
D = 80 cm, B = 44 cm—OK?
D = 120 cm, B = 66 cm—OK?
OK.
OK.
OK.

So, something's not right.
What about the scale?
Did you count by 10s?
Yep!

No, you didn't!
Look, when you got to 100
you started counting by 20s!
Gosh, I must have
looked at that ten times!
I guess that's why
someone else should look!

That's why they say
two heads are better
than one.
Now my graph looks
like yours, so we are
both correct!

How's everything going?
Hi, Mrs. Graham.

Our predictions weren't the same. So we knew there was something wrong.
We looked at it again and figured it out together. Is that OK?

Great! That's the way scientists and mathematicians do it. They get together and help each other out by questioning, comparing, and thinking.

Better that you should find the mistake than me. That's the way you learn.
It was like solving a mystery— "The Case of the Mistaken Graph!"

Of course, when you checked your prediction the ball would have told you who was right!

It was more fun figuring it out first!
Right! Now, let's see. If the bounce height was one meter…

Journey to Flatopia

Prof. Peabody ends a hard day at work.
Hmm, I wish I could remember where I parked my car.
Try 500 meters ahead and 300 meters to the left.

I had better get to the sitter and pick up Sweet P.
VOLVOX
TIMS

After dinner …
Sweet P.,
your mom is out of town working on that mapping job with Mrs. Origin. Do you want to help me in the laboratory?

Professor Peabody is building a time machine …
DIMENSIONS
5
4
3
2
1
If I can get this to work, I'll be famous. I can solve some of the mysteries of history. Who discovered zero? When was the first calendar invented?

If this works, I'll be able to travel back in time by going through the fourth dimension.
DIMENSIONS
5
4
3
2
1

POW!
What???
POP!
ZAP
DIMENSIONS
5
4
3
RUN PROGRAM

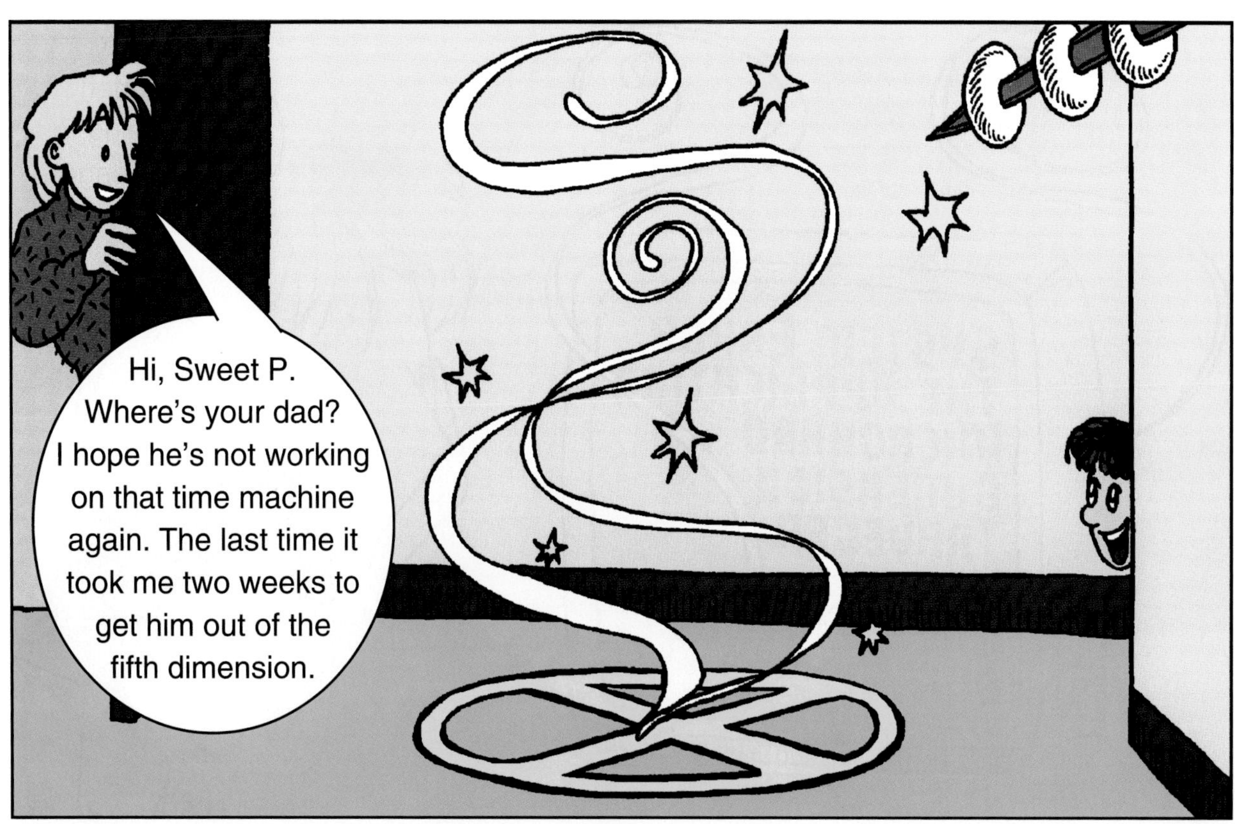
Hi, Sweet P.
Where's your dad?
I hope he's not working on that time machine again. The last time it took me two weeks to get him out of the fifth dimension.

In Service
and
Busy...
Back Soon.
Uh-oh.

SYSTEM ERROR.
THE APPLICATION
MICROHARD
DIMENSION
TRAVELER
HAS
UNEXPECTEDLY
QUIT.
Good grief!
This is going to
be a challenge.

The next day.
Well, I think I've got the
communicator repaired.
Here's a letter from your dad.

Dear Pat and Sweet P.,

I guess you're wondering where I am. It seems that the time machine works, but not in the way I planned. When I first arrived here, I realized that something was very odd. Two shapes approached me, one orange and the other green. "Stranger," said the green shape, "we saw you appear from nowhere. Who are you and how did you come to be here?"

"I'm Professor Peabody," I replied, "and I believe I have come here accidentally in my multidimensional travel machine. I was trying to travel through time by using the fourth dimension." "What a bogus story," replied the orange shape. "Everyone knows that there's no such thing as the fourth dimension. Even the third dimension is an invention of science-fiction writers. Sane people know there are only two dimensions in the real world." I finally realized that I must have been transported to a two-dimensional world.

"Come closer, stranger, so we can count your vertices," said the green shape. The shapes came close to me and I could tell that the orange shape had four sides that were of equal length and four right angles. The green shape had three sides of equal length. They started feeling my shape.

"Yaaaaaagh, it's ugly," said the first. "It's horrible," said the second. "Let's get out of here before we get sick." And with that, the two shapes moved away as fast as they could.

I spent the next day trying to talk to these creatures, but they always fled in terror. Finally, I found one that would talk to me. "Stranger, is it true that you come from a world of three dimensions?" it said. "Yes. I'm glad I have found someone at last who will speak to me," I said gratefully.

The shape spoke to me again. "I am Isabel Newton, head scientist of Flatopia. My mathematical theories predicted that there could be a three-dimensional world, but everyone in Flatopia thinks my theories are crazy. I was banished from Flatopia for teaching my students about three and four dimensions."

"Why are the beings here so afraid of me?" I asked.

"All living things in Flatopia are polygons," she said. "Flatopia beings think beauty is symmetry—the more lines of symmetry, the more beautiful. Also we think that the more vertices you have, the more important you are. You appear to have no vertices at all, and your sides are not line segments. Flatopians think you are very strange and ugly."

Dr. Newton then went on to tell me about Flatopia society. If two beings meet on the street, each one moves around the other and counts its vertices. The one with fewer vertices must move aside to let the other one pass. When both beings have the same number of vertices, the one with fewer lines of symmetry must move out of the way. For example, a nonsquare rectangle will have to move out of the way of a square. If two beings with the same number of sides and lines of symmetry meet, they will often have a nasty quarrel about who has the right of way.

All the farmers in Flatopia are right triangles. There are two kinds of right triangles, left-facing triangles (called Lefties) and right-facing triangles (called Righties).

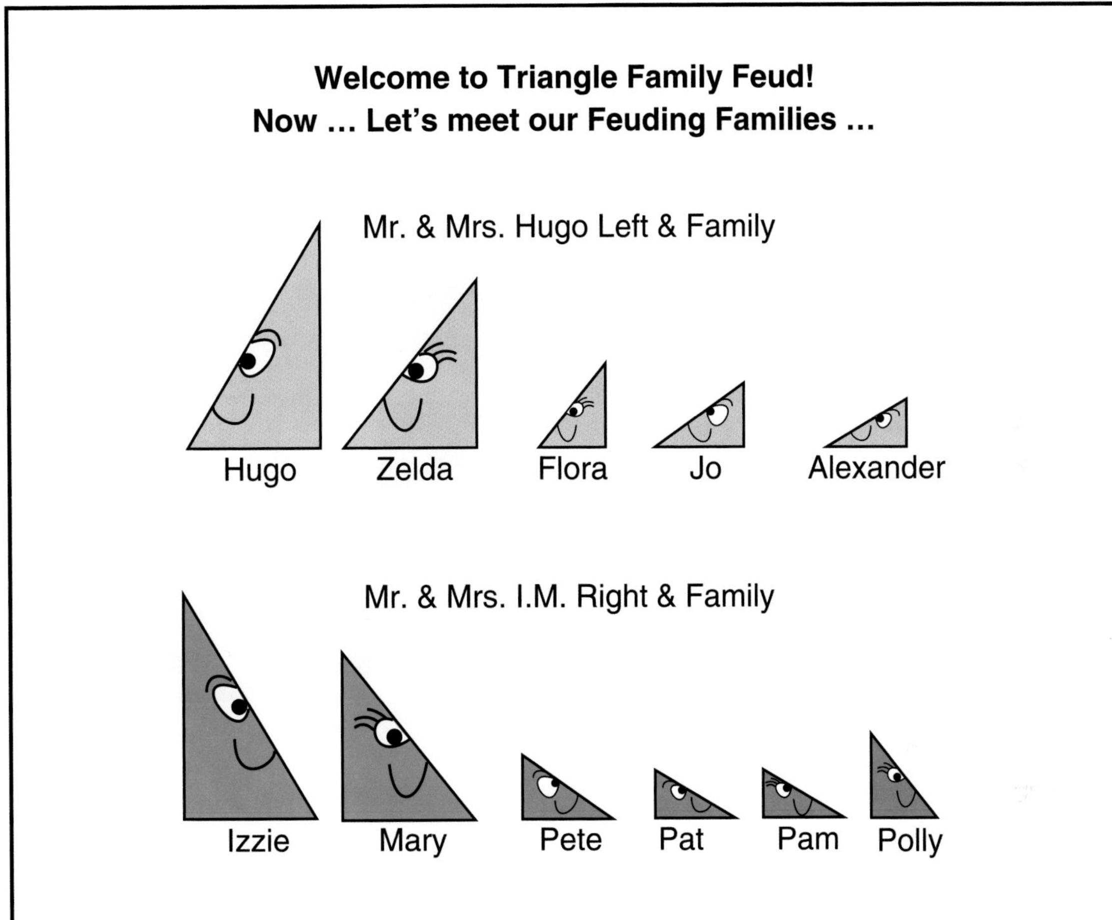

For centuries, the Righties and Lefties have been feuding. Since they are always fighting, they do not spend enough time growing crops. Now there is a food shortage in Flatopia. Strangely enough, no one remembers how this feud began and no one can think of a way to end it.

As Dr. Newton was explaining this to me, I noticed that some beings were approaching us. After feeling their sides and vertices, I could tell that they were all squares. "Horrible creature," they said to me, "His Majesty King Deka X commands that you stop speaking with the troublemaker, Dr. Newton, and come immediately to his castle." This was said in a most unfriendly tone, so I began to worry about my safety.

"King Deka thinks he is the most powerful and symmetric person in the world," said Dr. Newton. "He has the largest number of sides in the kingdom, 10, and is a regular polygon. So he has 10 lines of symmetry." "Stop talking to this creature, Dr. Newton," said the captain of the squares. "You've made enough trouble already, filling people's heads with fairy tales about a three-dimensional world. Clap them in chains!" With this command, I was surrounded by squares and Dr. Newton and I were escorted to the royal court.

As soon as the captain told the king about my arrival and my conversation with Dr. Newton, the king shouted, "Off with his head! Heretics must be punished!" "But, Your Majesty," I shouted, "I can prove that there is a three-dimensional world." The queen turned to the king and said, "This creature is amusing. Let's hear what it has to say, dear." "Hrrumph!" grumbled the king. "Let the madman speak."

"Most wise King," I said, "since your world is two-dimensional, you cannot see a three-dimensional object." "Obviously," replied the king. "Now," I said, "I will show a three-dimensional object called a sphere, but we will only be able to see two-dimensional slices called circles."

Then I used the tractor beam on my time machine to move a sphere into Flatopia. "Here is the first part of the sphere, Your Majesty," I said.

"Why, that's nothing but a point!" he said. "Are you trying to make a fool out of me?"

The sphere touches Flatopia—the view from Flatopia

The sphere touches Flatopia—the view from our 3-D world

"Hush, dear," admonished the queen. "Let him continue." I then started moving the sphere through Flatopia. The shapes gasped with pleasure as they saw the point turn into a circle that became larger and larger. "It's beautiful!"

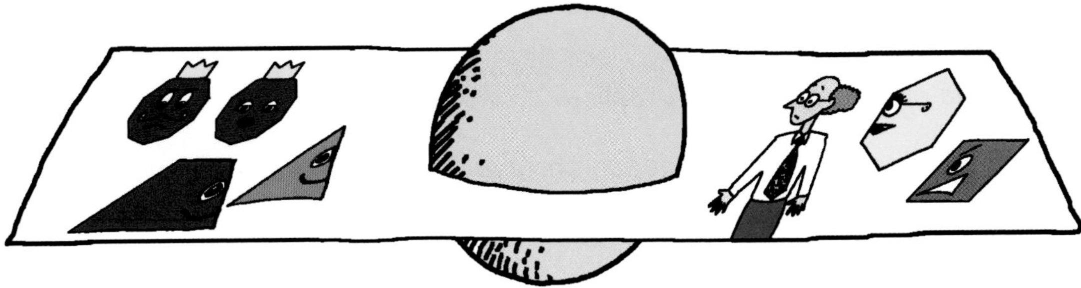

The sphere passes through Flatopia

One person even whispered, "It's more symmetrical than the king!" The king said, "Evil creature, do you dare insult the King by creating a shape with more than 10 lines of symmetry? Off with his head!" I looked at the king and said, "Most gracious majesty, it is true that this shape, which is called a circle, has many lines of symmetry. In fact, any line through the center is a line of symmetry. So, there are an infinite number of lines of symmetry. But this shape can be the symbol of your family, a reminder of your infinite wisdom and beauty."

"Well, since you put it that way, I see that you are a most sensible and reasonable creature," the king replied. "Continue!"

"Notice that as the sphere passes through Flatopia, the circle grows, but now it is starting to shrink," I said. As we watched, the circle got smaller and smaller until it became a point once more. Then the point disappeared.

With this, the queen turned to me and said, "Most noble creature, we are amazed by what you have shown us. Who would have guessed that a three-dimensional world could exist? We hereby welcome you to Flatopia and make you an honorary citizen." "And, as for you, Dr. Newton," said the king, "we welcome you back to our kingdom. Let bygones be bygones. In fact, we would like you to be the Royal Scientific Advisor."

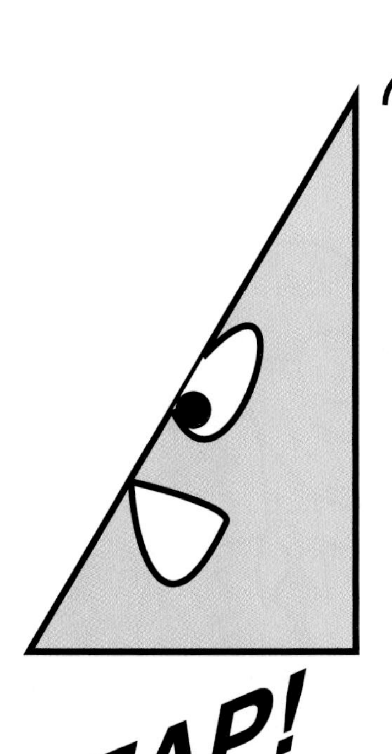

Then the king said, "Well, science may be good and useful to know, but it cannot solve our most serious problem: the right-triangle feud."

"But, Sire," I said, "this is one problem that science can solve." I looked around and found a left-facing right triangle waiting in the back of the room. "Let me use my special reflectorizer to flip this triangle fellow."

"What happened to me?" he cried. "I was a Lefty . . . and now I'm a Righty!"

"Don't you see," I said, "all right triangles are created equal. There's really no difference between left-facing triangles and right-facing triangles because I can use the third dimension to flip one into the other."

So here I am, my dear, enjoying fame and fortune in Flatopia. But I miss you and Sweet P. very much and hope that you will find a way to get me back home soon.

At least your father is safe.
Let's fix this machine and get him back.

END PROGRAM
DIMENSIONS
5
4
3
POW!
Yikes!
POP!
ZAP

That was great, Dad.
Can we come with you and explore
a four-dimensional world now?

Gulp!
I don't think I'm ready for another trip just yet.
Let's plan our next trip *before* we go!

Alberto in TenthsLand

Alberto was reading a book in the library when it happened. The book was about basketball, Alberto's favorite game, but Alberto had played basketball all morning, and he was feeling sleepy and dull. He had begun to wonder how high a basketball would bounce if it were dropped from the rim, 10 feet up. He didn't know how he could find out since he couldn't reach that high to drop the ball. He thought the problem was like something he had done in school, but he couldn't remember exactly what.

Then he saw it. A small white mouse ran across the library floor and disappeared into a heating vent. Seeing a mouse was not unusual since the library was old. Alberto was not even especially surprised to see that this mouse was dressed in sweats and high-tops. But when the mouse pulled out a calculator and started pushing buttons furiously as he scurried along, Alberto jumped up and hurried after him.

After the mouse disappeared into the heating vent, Alberto paused hardly a moment before crawling in himself. He crawled down a tunnel for a few meters. Then, suddenly, he found himself falling down, down, down.

He fell for what seemed a very long time, but at last he landed gently on a pile of crumpled newspapers. He was just able to see the white mouse hurry off down a narrow path through the woods.

Alberto jumped up and started down the path after the white mouse. He hadn't gone far when he came to a clearing in the woods. He was just in time to see the white mouse disappear through a very small door in a tree.

Alberto hurried over to the door and kneeled down to take a peek. Through the door he saw a wonderful garden. Alberto was bitterly disappointed that he was far too big to fit through the door.

When Alberto stood up, he was surprised to see a strange machine in the clearing—he was sure it hadn't been there before. The machine looked like a small rocket launch pad with a tower. On the side of the tower was written "Ten-X-Sizer" and at the top was a button labeled "Push Me."

Alberto stood on the pad and looked at the button. Now, Alberto was always careful with machines, and he knew that pushing buttons could sometimes cause trouble, so he looked all around to see if there were any signs labeled "Danger." He found none, so he decided to push the button. The next thing Alberto knew his head was poking up past the tops of the trees all around and his feet were rapidly disappearing. "Good-bye, feet. Be good," thought Alberto as he grew and grew and grew.

The view from high above the trees was lovely, but now Alberto was farther than ever from being able to get through the tiny door and into the wonderful garden. The disappointment was too much for poor Alberto, and he began to cry. He sat down and shed huge tears.

After a few minutes of crying, Alberto noticed another machine in the clearing, and he wondered why he hadn't noticed this one before either. This machine was very much like the first machine; only the words on the tower were different. On the new machine was written, "Tenth-X-Sizer."

Alberto thought that he might as well try this machine too, as he figured he could be no worse off than he was already. It was hard for him to fit on the machine, but as soon as he pushed the button he felt himself shrinking, shrinking, shrinking. In a moment, he was back to his proper size.

"If one push can do so much," thought Alberto, "I wonder what another will do." Alberto pushed the Tenth-X-Sizer button again and to his delight found himself shrinking once more. Luckily, he did not shrink away to nothing, but stopped at just the perfect height to fit through the tiny door in the tree. Immediately, Alberto went through the door and found himself in the beautiful garden.

"Stop!" cried an odd creature who looked like a large piece of paper. "I am the Ten Percent Taxer. Pay your taxes at once or go to jail!"

"Taxes?" replied Alberto. "What are taxes?"

"Taxes buy civilization," answered the Ten Percent Taxer. "Now, show me what you have and I will take 10 percent. You must pay $\frac{1}{10}$ of what you have."

Alberto emptied his pockets. He had a bag of marbles, a quarter, a dime, four pennies, a half-empty package of chewing gum, and some kite string.

The Ten Percent Taxer studied Alberto's treasure for a long time. At last he said, "We have determined your taxes. You owe two marbles, all four pennies, one stick of gum, and one-tenth of the kite string. You can keep the bag for the other marbles. Do you have a ruler?"

"I don't have a ruler, sorry," answered Alberto. "But, please, would you explain again why I must give you my stuff?"

"Paying taxes is the law. Taxes pay for schools, roads, police officers, and firefighters. Besides, if you don't pay your taxes, you'll go to jail," said the Ten Percent Taxer. "I'll just have to take all the string to the Centimeter Ruler. She'll help me figure out what 10 percent of it is."

"Who is the Centimeter Ruler?" asked Alberto.

"She's the queen of TenthsLand," answered the Ten Percent Taxer. Then he grabbed the string, two of the marbles, the pennies, and a stick of gum. He popped the gum in his mouth and hurried off.

Alberto gathered up his other things and looked around. He was startled to see what looked like a large caterpillar on the branch of a nearby tree. It seemed that the creature had been watching for some time.

"Who are you?" asked the creature.

"I'm not quite sure," answered Alberto. "I know who I was this morning when I got up, but I've changed several times since then, and now I'm not sure anymore. Who are you?"

"I'm the Tenth-i-Pede," replied the creature, who was beginning to disappear. The last three tenths were already gone and several more were fading fast. "If you don't know who you are, do you at least know what you're doing?"

Alberto answered, "I'm trying to find the white mouse. Have you seen him?"

"White mouse?" repeated the Tenth-i-Pede, who by this time was almost entirely gone. "White mouse? Look for the Centimeter Ruler. The white mouse works for her." And with that, the Tenth-i-Pede faded away the rest of the way, except for a faint outline of his smile, which lingered a minute or two longer.

But Alberto didn't have to look for the Centimeter Ruler after all. She was hurrying towards him now with the white mouse and the Ten Percent Taxer by her side.

"There he is, Your Majesty!" cried the Ten Percent Taxer. "It's his string."

"I have measured your string," said the Centimeter Ruler. "It was 237 cm long. Do you know what 10 percent of 237 cm is?"

"No, Your Majesty," answered Alberto.

"Mr. Mouse! Quickly, what's 10 percent of 237 cm?" shouted the Centimeter Ruler. "In the meantime, tell me how tall you are. I need to know to the nearest tenth of a centimeter."

"I'm sorry, Your Majesty," answered Alberto, "but I don't know that either."

"Come here, stand next to me!" shouted the Centimeter Ruler. "Now, Mr. Mouse, how tall is he?"

"About 24 cm," answered the white mouse.

"You ninny! He's nowhere near 24 cm!" shouted the Centimeter Ruler.

"I meant to say that 10 percent of the string is about 24 cm," answered the mouse. "This fellow looks about 15.6 cm tall."

"Now, that's more like it!" shouted the Centimeter Ruler. "Now, you, Ten Percent Taxer, get his shirt and pants—we need 10 percent of those too."

At that, the Ten Percent Taxer and the Centimeter Ruler began to grab Alberto's shirt, trying to pull it off.

"No! No!" shouted Alberto. "That's my shirt. Leave me alone!"

The Centimeter Ruler, the Ten Percent Taxer, and the white mouse all tugged and pulled at Alberto's shirt. Alberto gave a shout of anger and tried to beat them off. Then he found himself sitting back in the library. Mrs. Carroll, the librarian, was gently shaking his shoulder. "Wake up! Alberto, wake up!" she said. "You've been asleep for a very long time. You must go now; we're closing."

“Oh! What an amazing dream!” said Alberto as he gathered his books and hurried home to tell his mother about his strange dream.

Mrs. Carroll shook her head and smiled. Then, as she was closing up for the night, she saw a small white mouse scurry into an old heat vent. “How odd,” she thought, “for a moment it looked as though that mouse was wearing sweats and high-tops.”

Phil and Howard's Excellent Egyptian Adventure

It was a warm spring afternoon. Mrs. Dewey put a multiplication problem on the board and asked the class to solve it.

After school, Howard and Phil sat down to work on the homework problems that Mrs. Dewey assigned.
Let's see, here's the first problem: One type of airplane can hold 21 passengers. How many passengers could 14 of these planes hold?
Maybe Professor Peabody can show us. Let's go over to his laboratory and ask him.
I wonder if there are more ways to do these problems.

Howard and Phil arrived at Professor Peabody's, eager to see what was going on in the laboratory behind his house.
Hi, Professor. Howard and I were hoping you could help us with our multiplication. We're looking for different ways to solve problems.
Well, kids, come on in. You got here just in time! I was just warming up my time machine for another test. I think I have it fixed now so I won't get stuck in another dimension.

I'll bet I know just the person to help you out with multiplication. How would you like to visit ancient Egypt?
Wow, that sounds great!
Oh, wait a minute, I have all this homework and Mom expects me home for dinner by 5:00 P.M. sharp.
No problem. A visit in this time machine should only take a minute. Hop in, we'll be back before we're missed.

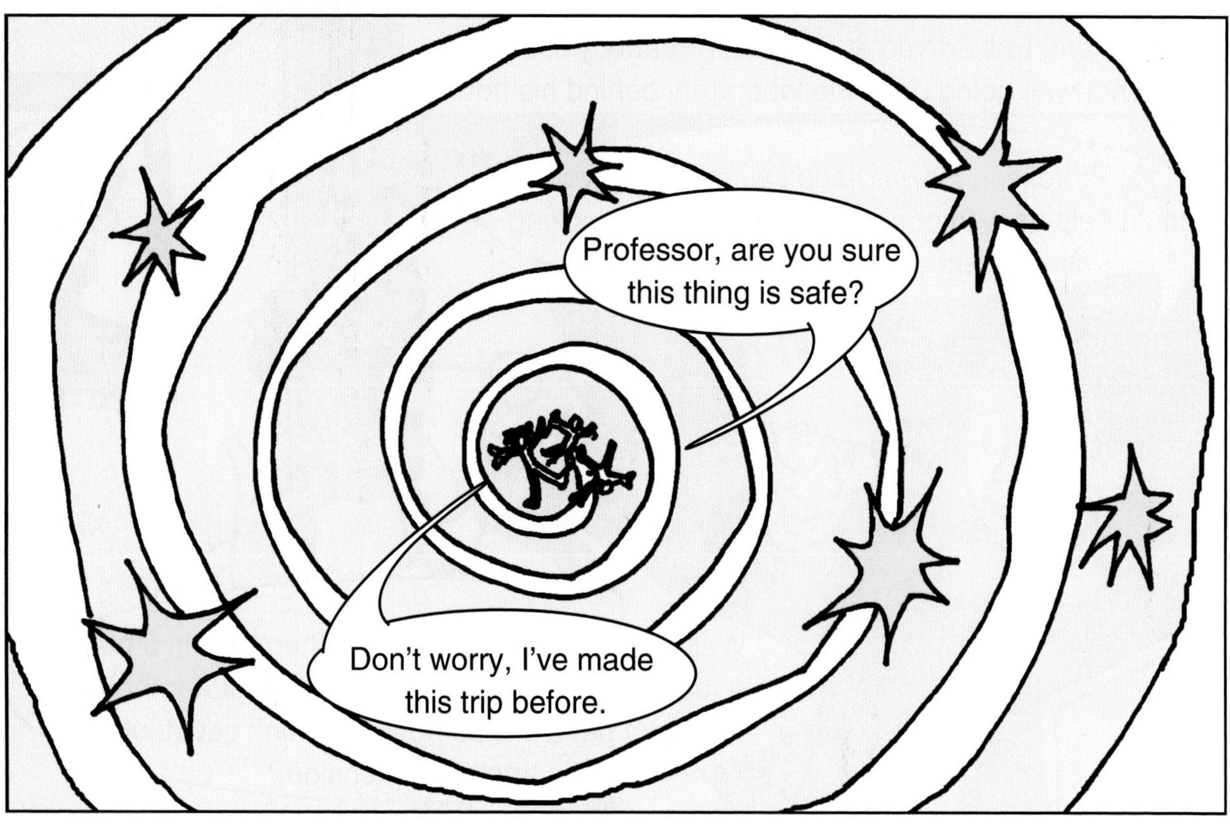
Professor, are you sure this thing is safe?
Don't worry, I've made this trip before.

Wow, where are we?
If my calculations are correct, we are in a room of King Chefren's palace in about 2550 BCE. If we're lucky, we should be able to find some help for your multiplication problem.

Ah yes, here he is. Meet an old friend, Ka-Irw-Khufu. He is one of the Pharaoh's most honored scribes.

Ahh, it is the mysterious Professor with the strange clothes. And who are your most honored small companions?
Hello, my friend. It is good to see you again. These are my assistants, Howard and Phil. I am training them to be mathematicians. Today, I have brought them to you for instruction in duplation.
I would be most honored to share my calculating methods with Professor Howard and Professor Phil.

Do you know hieroglyphics?
No, what are they?
They are the special symbols that stand for words in the records we keep for the Pharaoh. When they are carved in stone, they look like little pictures. Special artists carve and paint the story of our Pharaoh's life on the walls of his tomb. That way, the gods will know his greatest deeds when his spirit travels down the Nile to meet them.

How do you make the numbers?
When we count small groups, we make a stroke for each group like this.

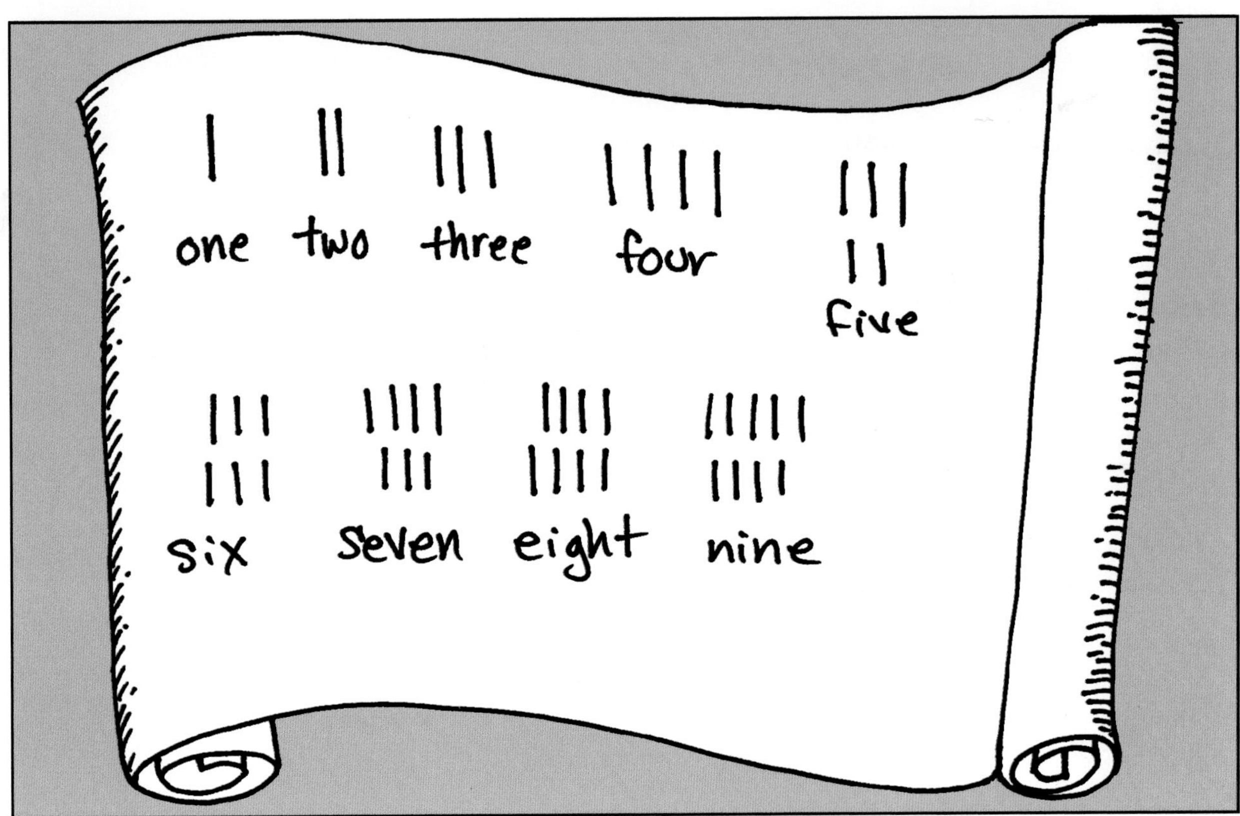
one
two
three
four
five
six
seven
eight
nine

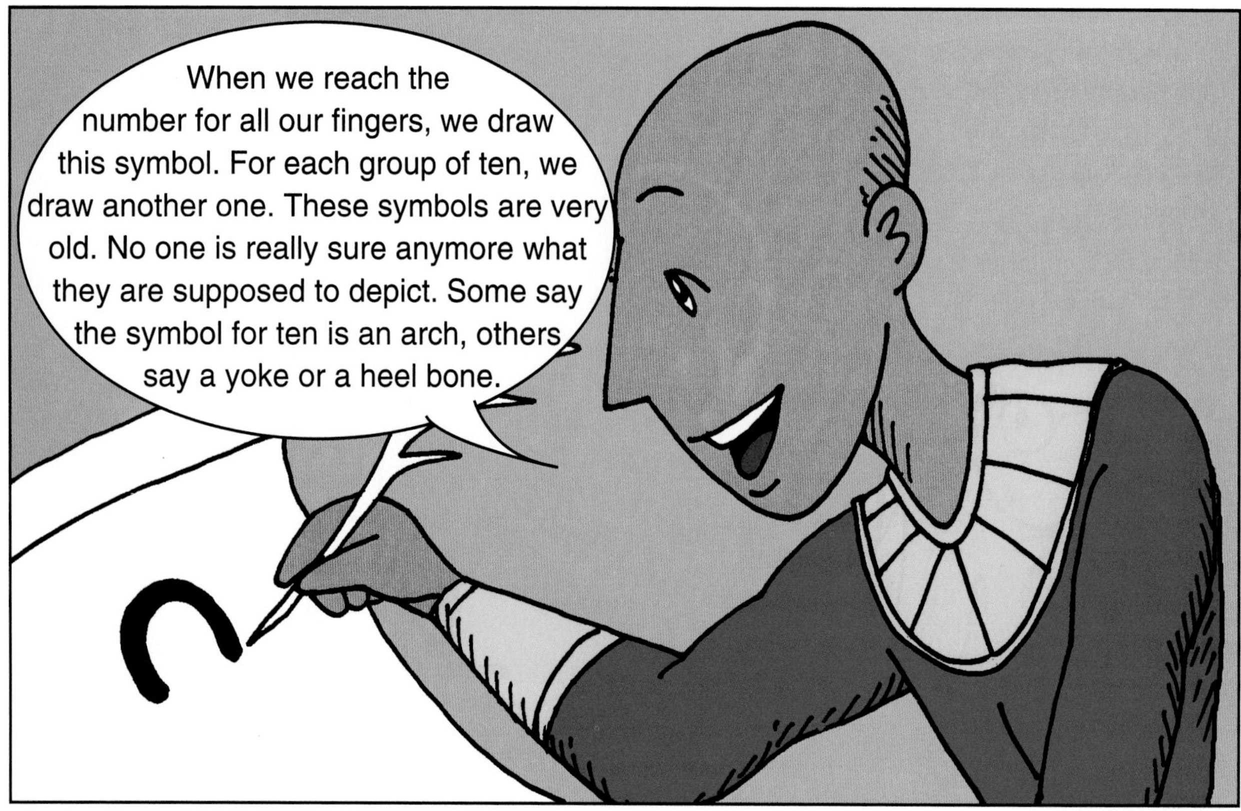
When we reach the number for all our fingers, we draw this symbol. For each group of ten, we draw another one. These symbols are very old. No one is really sure anymore what they are supposed to depict. Some say the symbol for ten is an arch, others say a yoke or a heel bone.

Professor Peabody showed me the strange method you have for writing numbers. The symbol we use for ten tens, or one hundred, looks like a coil of rope.
10
100

We draw a lotus flower for each group of one thousand, while ten thousand is shown by a bent finger.
10
100
1000
10,000

For one hundred thousand, this is the symbol that is used. It may be a tadpole, a burbot fish from the Nile River, or a bird. The symbol for one million is the figure of a person or a god.
100,000
1,000,000

So, if I want to write the number three thousand, five hundred, twenty-seven I would do it like this?
Yes, that is correct.

This is really great, but how will it help me to get my multiplication problems done before 5 o'clock?
What is this 5 o'clock?
Never mind, Ka. Can you show Howard how you solve problems? If you had 14 boats that each carry 21 jars of oil, how can you find the number of jars of oil there are on all the boats?

I would simply make a number table by doubling, starting with 21. Then, I would double 21, which is 42. The double of 42 is 84. (That is four times 21.) Then, I would double 84, which is 168. So, 168 is 8 × 21.

$1 \times 21 = 21$

$2 \times 21 = 42$

$4 \times 21 = 84$

$8 \times 21 = 168$

Now, I can use my table to find the total number of jars of oil. When I add eight and four and two the total is 14, so I can add the total of those doubles from my table. I just combine all those numbers. That means that there are 294 jars of oil on the boats.

Since 2 + 4 + 8 = 14, then 14 × 21 is 42 + 84 + 168 = 294.

$1 \times 21 = 21$

$8 + 4 + 2 = 14$ — $2 \times 21 = 42$, $4 \times 21 = 84$, $8 \times 21 = 168$ — $42 + 84 + 168 = 294$

I see it's really easy to double using hieroglyphics. You just write the number twice. So, the double of 84 is 168.
Yes, but when you write the double, you have to gather together groups of ones and write a ten instead. So, 84 doubled looks like this instead of this.
That is just like we do in our system when we regroup.

How do you write zero in hieroglyphics?
What is a zero?
It is the way to write nothing.
If you have nothing, why would you want to write anything?

Since the Egyptians used different symbols for one, ten, one hundred, etc., they never needed a symbol to show zero.
When I write two hundred and four (204), if I leave out the zero in the middle, everyone will think I mean twenty-four instead. The zero helps me to show that the two is in the hundreds' place. But the Egyptians did not need a zero to write two hundred and four.
204

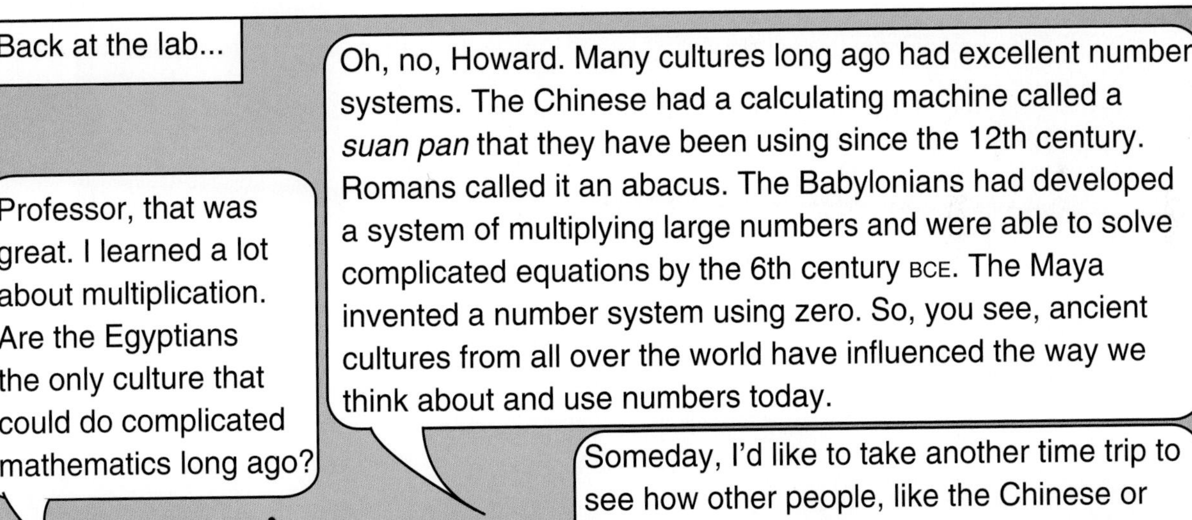
Back at the lab...
Professor, that was great. I learned a lot about multiplication. Are the Egyptians the only culture that could do complicated mathematics long ago?
Oh, no, Howard. Many cultures long ago had excellent number systems. The Chinese had a calculating machine called a *suan pan* that they have been using since the 12th century. Romans called it an abacus. The Babylonians had developed a system of multiplying large numbers and were able to solve complicated equations by the 6th century BCE. The Maya invented a number system using zero. So, you see, ancient cultures from all over the world have influenced the way we think about and use numbers today.
Someday, I'd like to take another time trip to see how other people, like the Chinese or the Maya, used numbers to solve problems.

The next day in school...
14 x 21 =
1 x 21 = 21
2 x 21 = 42
4 x 21 = 84
8 x 21 = 168
168 + 84 + 42 =
294
My goodness, Phil. That method does work. How did you figure it out?
Well, a very old friend showed it to me.

Now, let's review division.
5⟌214
Uh-oh. I think we may be paying Ka another visit!

Prob$_e$ Quest

Suzanne and Joe are twins. Their favorite pastime is playing the video game *Prob$_e$ Quest.* They sit for hours at a time in front of the video monitor, challenged by harder and harder levels of play. In the game, each twin controls a space probe. The goal of the game is to be the first to reach the outer planet of the solar system. The levels of the game are based on the planets players conquer. The master of the game is a character named SOL. Players meet many obstacles along the way, from mysterious creatures to black holes.

One beautiful day during spring vacation, Suzanne and Joe's mother found them again sitting in front of the video monitor.

"I want you two to go outside and find your friends. It's too nice a day to be sitting inside like this. I'm going on some errands. Your brother is here if you need anything. Now, go outside!" ordered Mom.

"Yes, Mom," the twins answered.

Another hour passed with the twins still sitting in front of the monitor.

"I thought Mom said you were going outside! What are you still doing in here?" asked the twins' older brother, Mike, as he entered the living room. "Get a life!"

The twins spent the rest of the day playing the game.

Turn the page.

That night, after the twins were asleep in their rooms, a tremendous spring storm passed through the area. A loud, window-shaking clap of thunder awoke Suzanne. She couldn't get back to sleep so she decided to go into the living room where she could play *Prob$_e$ Quest.* Joe soon joined her and the game began.

Suddenly, a bright bolt of lightning seemed to leap into the room, followed immediately by a roar of thunder. The twins were knocked to the floor and the monitor went blank. When the monitor came back on, the twins were nowhere to be seen.

"Where are we?" asked Suzanne.

"I don't know. It sure doesn't look like our living room!" replied Joe. "Wait a minute, our living room is out there. Look through the glass. We're inside the game! Something weird must have happened when we hit the floor."

"How do we get back? I'm scared," cried Suzanne.

"Me too! Look, I found something," said Joe.

Joe picked up an object. "It looks like an 'e.' I wonder where it came from?"

Turn the page.

"Look! SOL is coming toward us. What's happening?" asked Suzanne.

"Welcome to *Prob Quest,*" said SOL.

Both the twins began to talk at once. "How did we get here?"

"How do we get back out there?"

"What's *Prob Quest?* Weren't we playing *Prob$_e$ Quest?*"

"Be silent!" commanded SOL. "Everything has changed, nothing is as it should be. It is possible for you to return to your home only by playing *Prob Quest.*"

"But what is *Prob Quest*?" asked Joe, panicking. "How can we play if we don't know what it is?"

"Silence!" yelled SOL. "I told you nothing is as it should be. The lightning caused all this to happen. You were consumed by the game and, at the same time, the game itself was changed. Look at the corner of the screen. The game you were playing was *Prob$_e$ Quest.* Now, the name of the game you are playing is *Prob Quest.*"

"I don't understand. What is 'Prob'?" asked Suzanne.

"Silence! For now you need only to listen. 'Prob' stands for probability. And I trust you know what probability means. Look around. Do you recognize your location?"

Turn the page.

"Look at all the rings. We must be on Level Six, Saturn. We're three levels away from home—I mean Earth. SOL, please explain how we can get home," pleaded Joe.

"To return 'home,' as you put it, you must correctly solve questions about probability until you return to Level Three. But, BE AWARE! An incorrect answer could send you hurtling into a black hole from which you can never return."

"We studied probability in school. If we work together, I'm sure we'll be home in no time," said Suzanne.

"I hope so," whispered Joe.

Your job is to help the twins on their journey home. Each time they are presented with a new quest, you need to choose the path they are to follow.

Turn the page.

The Quest for Level Five

SOL began to speak again, “Let us begin your journey. Each time a quest is presented, you will be given three possible answers. Choose correctly and you will find yourselves a level closer to home. Choose incorrectly and . . .”

“We may never see our home again. We understand,” said Suzanne, her voice shaking. “Please begin.”

“Look at the circle over there. Do you recognize it?” asked SOL.

“It looks like a probability spinner. We studied those in school,” replied Joe.

“Exactly! Examine it closely, and consider your first quest. What is the probability of a spin landing in the green area?”

Choose the response you think the twins should make, then follow the instructions.

(1) The same as spinning “red.” Turn to page 82.

(2) One-half. Turn to page 84.

(3) One chance in three. Turn to page 83.

The Quest for Level Four

The twins found themselves on Jupiter, which had served as Level Five of *Probe Quest.*

“Wow, this is amazing! It feels as if there is nothing below us, but I see something,” exclaimed Suzanne.

“Don’t you remember? We learned in school that some astronomers think Jupiter is just made up of gases and is not solid at all,” reminded Joe. “Let’s get out of here as fast as we can!”

Suddenly, out of the gases surrounding the children, appeared a creature known as CUBE. The creature was blank on every side, able to change its appearance, as the children would soon see.

“So, you have made it to my level. I wonder if you have the strength left to meet the next quest I am about to set forth.” The voice seemed to come from within the creature.

“Of course we do!” said Suzanne.

“Please, can we just get started?” asked Joe.

“So eager, my young friends. Very well, we shall begin. Observe closely.”

Before the astonished eyes of the children, one eye began to appear on a face of CUBE. Two eyes appeared on another face, three eyes on yet another face.

“CUBE is becoming a number cube like we used in school!” exclaimed Suzanne.

“A very clever observation. I have transformed myself into a fair number cube. Do you understand what that means? Every side has an equal chance of appearing. I am going to roll 10 times.”

“I think we had better keep track of the rolls, just as we did in school,” suggested Joe.

Turn the page.

At the end of the 10 rolls, Joe reported that a 1 had appeared three times, a 2 had appeared one time, a 3 two times, a 5 three times, and a 6 once. A 4 was never rolled.

"Very interesting information," said CUBE. "But can you use it to answer this question, 'How likely is the next roll to be a 4?'"

Choose the response you think the twins should make, then follow the instructions.

(1) It will not be a 4. Turn to page 86.

(2) The chances are one in six. Turn to page 85.

(3) It is very likely it will be a 4. Turn to page 86.

The Quest for Level Three: Home

The children found themselves standing on what looked like red soil. Joe recalled that Mars is sometimes referred to as the "red planet."

"Well, if this is Mars, we are definitely closer to home," said Joe.

"I wonder what our next quest will be. Oh, no! Look! Here comes TOWERING TWO HEADS. He's the creature I hate the most!" cried Suzanne.

TOWERING TWO HEADS was an awesome-looking creature. He appeared to be 100 feet tall. The two heads were very different from one another. One had a face shaped like a square. The other had a face shaped like a triangle. Because TOWERING TWO HEADS was known for his trickery, he was one of the most feared creatures in the game.

"Ah! Children, we were told to expect your arrival. Welcome to our level!" said the square head. The two heads knocked together with excitement.

"Yes, we are looking forward to your staying with us a long, long time," added the triangle face. Again, the two heads knocked together.

"But we can't stay here! We need to get back home. Our family will worry," said Suzanne.

"Please, just give us our quest so that we can be on our way," said Joe.

Turn the page.

"We find your impatience irritating. You do not deserve to spend time in this honorable place. Look, over there." TOWERING TWO HEADS pointed to an area of the sky where a line was gradually appearing. "Do you recognize that which is appearing before you?"

"It looks like a probability line," answered Suzanne.

"Ah, yes. And just what is a 'probability line'?" asked the triangle face.

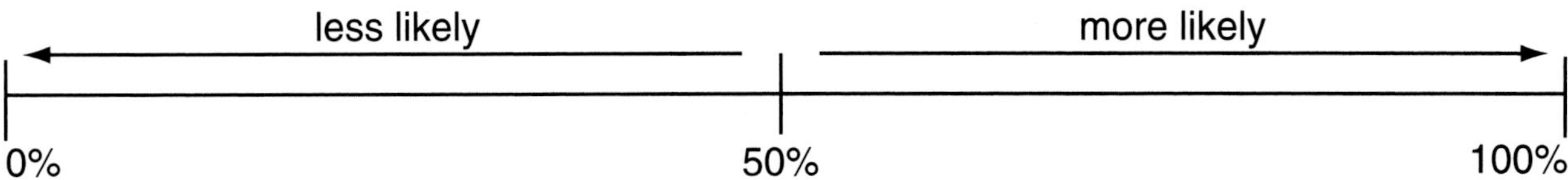

"It's a way of showing how likely something is to happen. If something is at the left end of the line, it cannot happen. If something is at the right end of the line, it will positively happen. There is room between the ends of the line for stuff that is not impossible or certain," answered Joe.

Turn the page.

"Let us see if you can use your knowledge of this line to help you in your last quest. We are the tallest of all that exists. However, we understand there is a game often played by some tall people who reside on Level Three. It is called basketball. You are familiar with this game? We see by your nodding heads that you are. We also understand that there are men who play in something called the National Basketball Association. This is true? We see again from your nods that it is. Listen carefully. If you meet an NBA player, what is the probability that he is at least 6 feet 2 inches tall? Place this probability on the probability line."

Choose the response you think the twins should make, then follow the instructions.

(1) 100%. Turn to page 87.

(2) Very likely. Turn to page 89.

"You should have looked more closely at the size of the three different areas," said SOL. "Sadly, you have chosen incorrectly. However, I am a merciful Game Master. I will give you one more chance to answer this quest correctly."

Return to page 76 and choose from the options remaining. If this was your second incorrect guess, turn to page 88.

An angry SOL began to speak, “You have answered this quest unwisely. You were fooled by the fact that the circle is divided into three parts. However, the three parts do not have the same area. Since you are inexperienced at *Prob Quest,* I will allow you to think again about the problem before you. I warn you, another incorrect answer will cause you to disappear into a black hole, from which there is no return.”

Return to page 76 and choose from the options remaining. If this was your second incorrect guess, turn to page 88.

"The answer to the quest is indeed one-half. You have thought this out well. Because the green area makes up one-half of the area of the circle, it is to be expected that a spinner would land there one-half of the time," explained SOL.

"Does this mean we can move one level closer to home now?" asked Suzanne.

"You promised that if we answered correctly, we would," chimed in Joe.

"Are you questioning the word of SOL? You will move to Level Five. However, be aware, for an even greater challenge awaits you there. Now, BE GONE!"

In less than the blink of an eye, the twins found themselves on Level Five, one step closer to home.

Turn to page 77 to continue the quest.

Prob Quest

CUBE began speaking. “You have studied probability well. Because I am a 6-sided shape, there is a one in six chance for a 4 to appear each time I roll. There is also a five in six chance that a 4 will not appear. You have done well.”

“Does that mean we can move one level closer to home?” asked Suzanne.

“It does, indeed,” answered CUBE. And in less than a blink of an eye, the twins found themselves on Level Four, with only one quest standing between them and home.

Turn to page 79.

CUBE began speaking. "You did not recall what you have learned about number cubes. Remember, I am a fair number cube. All sides have the same probability of appearing on any roll. Simply the fact that 4 has not yet appeared changes nothing."

Turn to page 88.

"We knew we could trick you into thinking that all NBA players were at least 6 feet 2 inches tall. In fact, they are not. A few players are less than this height. This was not always true. In fact, just 50 of your years ago, only 50% of the players were taller than 6 feet 2 inches."

"What happens now?" asked Suzanne, tearfully.

"Are we never going to see our home again?" wondered Joe.

Turn to page 88.

SOL appeared, "You have not successfully met the challenge of the quest before you. We warned you of what could be the result of this. You are both destined to disappear into the black hole of space, never to be seen again."

The last sound the twins heard as they hurtled into space was the tapping caused by SOL's rays bouncing off each other as he shook his head.

Dear Readers,
Turn to page 90.

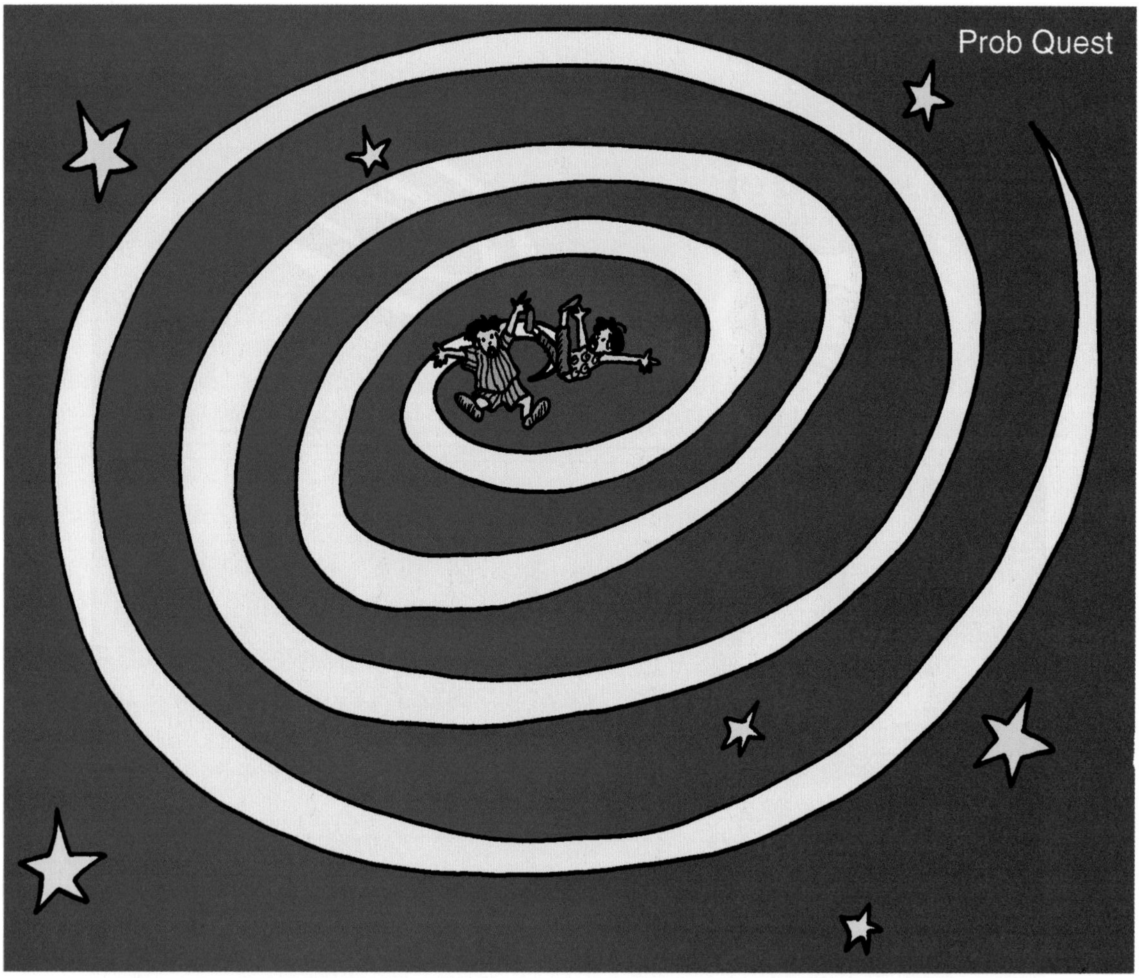

TOWERING TWO HEADS began, "We tried very hard to fool you, but by your thoughtful work, you have earned your way back home. Nearly every player in the NBA is taller than 6 feet 2 inches, but not all are."

In less than the blink of an eye, Suzanne and Joe found themselves once again in the living room of their own home.

"I have never been so afraid in my whole life!" said Joe.

"Me neither," said Suzanne. "I never thought we'd see our home again."

A branch could be heard, tapping loudly against the window.

Turn the page.

Joe and Suzanne were awakened the next morning by the sound of their mom and Mike tapping on their bedroom doors.

"Come on, get up. The two of you can't sleep the day away," said Mom.

The twins washed, put on their clothes, and went in to breakfast.

"I had the strangest dream last night, but I can't remember much about it," began Suzanne.

"Same here," said Joe. "It had something to do with the storm, I think."

"Well, the storm is long gone, and it's another beautiful day," said Mom. "I hope you two will go outside today instead of sitting in front of that computer."

Both of the children wandered into the living room and stood in front of the monitor.

"You know, I don't think I feel like playing the game today. Maybe I will go outside," said Joe.

"I'm with you," said Suzanne.

Just as the children went out the door, the computer monitor flashed to life. There, looking out of the screen stood SOL, CUBE, TOWERING TWO HEADS

and . . . MOM—smiling.

In the Shade of the Old Meranpi Tree

Over the Pacific Ocean, Dr. Clark and her son Todd are nearing Borneo. They are traveling to Borneo for the International Wildlife Association to study the rain forest.

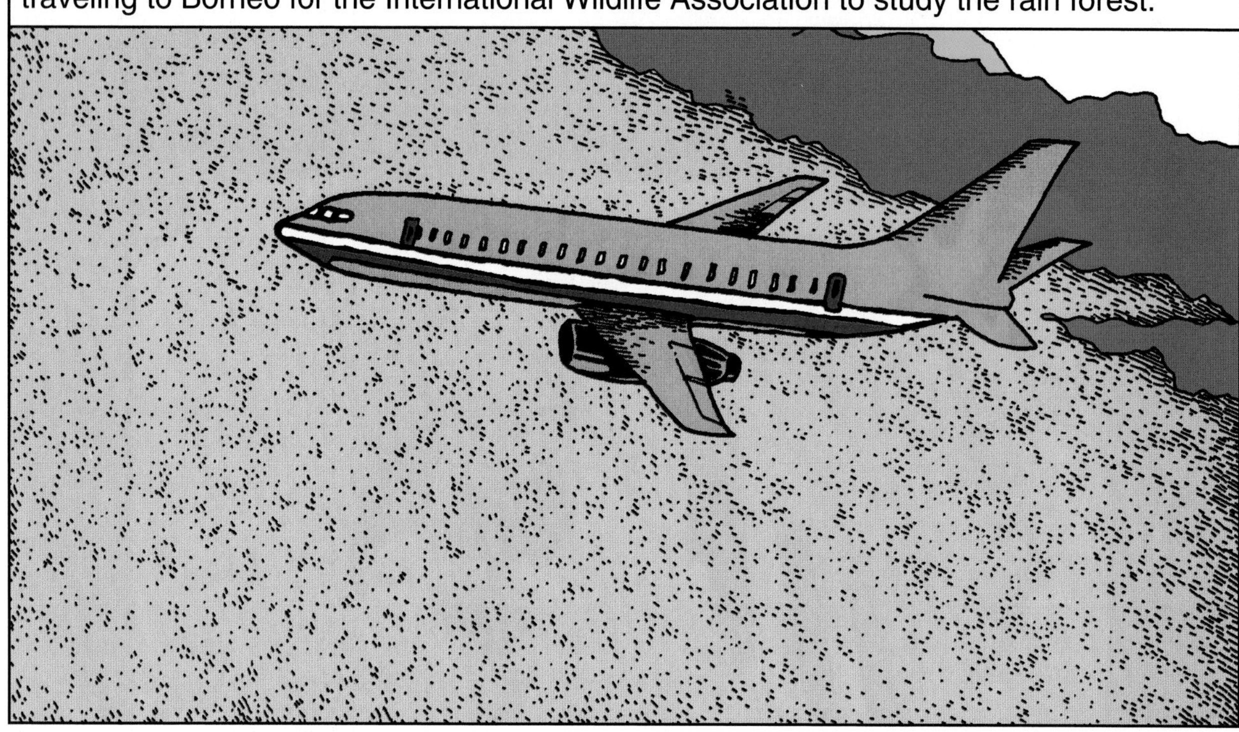

See the dark area along the equator? That's the tropical rain forest zone. There's Borneo.
Brazil and the Congos are also in the tropical rain forest zone.

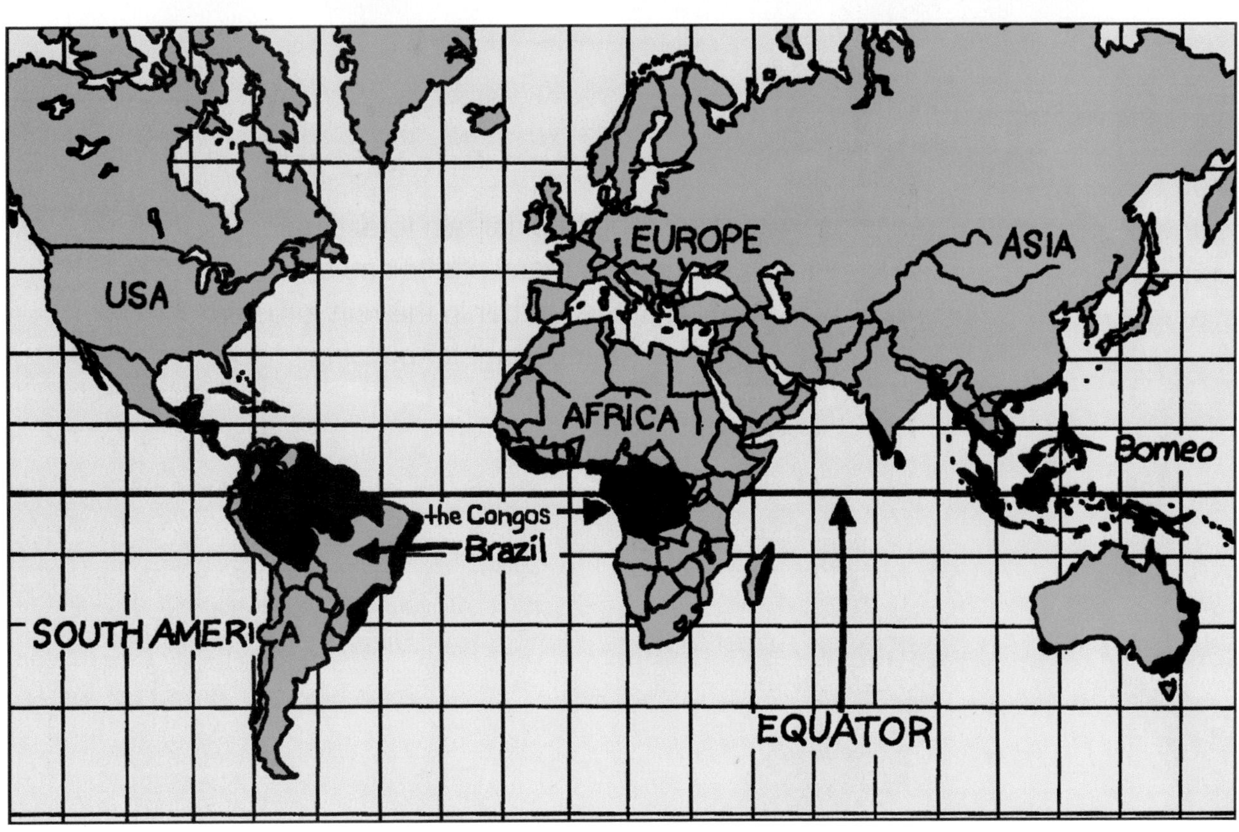
EUROPE
ASIA
USA
AFRICA
Borneo
the Congos
Brazil
SOUTH AMERICA
EQUATOR

As the plane banks over Borneo...
Look down there now. You can see what we're going to study.

The tropical rain forest zone supports many plants and animals. But, the lumber in the rain forest is important for building.

That area has been cleared out for timber. See the bald area and the road?

Won't cutting down the trees endanger the rain forest?

Possibly. That's why we're here—to study what happens if the loggers only cut the trees in a small area called a gap. Maybe new trees will grow back.
I sure hope so.
We need to study the size of the gap to see which size has the best conditions for new growth.

Later, at their campsite in the Danum Valley in North Borneo...
Look at the height of those trees. It's dark down here.
Those old meranpi trees are over 100 feet tall. They are so thick at the top, they cut off 98 percent of the light. It's these great old trees that are being logged.

Here are some seeds from the meranpi trees. They are all over the forest floor. See, they've germinated into seedlings. You can see the tap root and seed leaves, but it's so shady they hardly grow.
So, they need a lot of sun.

No, if they get too much sun, they dry out and die. Remember, seedlings need water to grow.
Not too hot, not too cold, not too dry, not too wet, just right.

That "just right" is what we've got to find out. If the gap size is too small, then there's not enough light. If the gap size is too big, then there is too much light. What is the "just right" gap size?
So, one of the important variables is gap size.

At this spot, the crew will cut down this meranpi tree that I'm marking. That should leave a gap in the canopy of about 200 square meters.

Later...
When we finish here, we'll move to another spot and mark two trees.
Right, and then to another spot and cut down four trees. Timber!

Later...
See the gap? It's about 200 square meters.
I can feel the sun. It's getting warmer already.

For each gap size, we want to measure seedling height versus time for three different kinds of trees.

Help mark the area with tags so we'll know which were measured. Red for the meranpi, yellow for the macaranga, and blue for the nervosa.
I get it. We'll see how gap size affects the growth of each species.

GAP AREA, ABOUT 200 SQUARE METERS

Nervosa

t in days	h in cm
0	18cm
14	
28	
42	

Meranpi

t in days	h in cm
0	2cm
14	
28	
42	

Macaranga

t in days	h in cm
0	
14	
28	
42	

The macaranga seed has not even started to grow yet. Record $H = 0$ for the macaranga. We'll see what the light does to it.
Shh...look.

It's a baby orangutan. We think birth rates of orangutans fall after logging. Dr. Sirrani is studying that.
It has no tail. And look at those arms. Its arm span must be twice its height.

During the next week, Dr. Clark and Todd set up and measure two more gap areas. After two weeks, they're back at the 200-square-meter gap.
It's a good thing we put on those tags!
The seedlings are all growing. Let's measure them.

The nervosa has grown to 27 centimeters. It's still the tallest.
But, the meranpi grew to 4 centimeters. And the macaranga is also 4 centimeters. It's caught up to the meranpi.

The next day at the two-tree gap site where the area of the gap is about 400 square meters...
Look at that. No more meranpi seedlings. Too much light. All we have are the shade-providing plants, the macaranga and nervosa.
So, the meranpi can't grow again in a gap this big.

Then, two weeks later, Dr. Clark and Todd are back at the one-tree gap site.
Hey, great! We still have meranpi seedlings.
The shade-providing plants are still the tallest. The macaranga's taller than the meranpi. Will the meranpi ever win out?

I think here it will because the meranpi have a good start. They are shaded by other trees. And in this forest the tallest trees are the meranpis. It may take 75 years. But, as yet, they haven't dried out.
The taller nervosa and macaranga will shade the meranpi, and they will get just the right amount of sunlight to grow tall.

That's the key. If the gap isn't too great, the other, faster-growing plants help them out, giving them the chance to grow.
But, when the meranpi grows tall, it will shade the others and they will die. That's not very nice after all the help it got.

It is a complicated problem. There are a lot of variables involved. In our experiment, we found that small gap sizes are better than large ones. We need to do more experiments to be sure we are correct and study other variables. It will take a lot of work to spare the rain forest.

And the orangutans, too.